The Jewish Museum
New York
November 23 through January 2, 1966

The Washington Gallery of Modern Art
Washington, D.C.
January 14 through February 20, 1966

2 Kinetic Sculptors

Nicolas Schöffer and Jean Tinguely

Introductory essays by
Jean Cassou,
K. G. Hultèn and
Sam Hunter
With a statement by
Nicolas Schöffer

October House Inc., New York

The Walker Art Center
Minneapolis, Minnesota
March 7 through April 10, 1966

The Carnegie Institute
Pittsburgh, Pennsylvania
April 28 through May 29, 1966

**The Contemporary Art Council
of the Seattle Art Museum**
Seattle, Washington
June 27 through July 31, 1966

Acknowledgments

I am indebted to the artists this catalogue describes, Nicolas Schöffer and Jean Tinguely, for their interest and cooperation, and wish also to express my grateful appreciation to the following for their varied and valued assistance: Mr. and Mrs. Jean de Menil, Niki de Saint-Phalle, Virginia Dwan, Alexandre Iolas, Naum Gabo, Rube Goldberg, Kynaston McShine, Sam Miller, Man Ray, Denise René, George Rickey, Mimi Shorr, Gordon Smith, Patsy Southgate and James Johnson Sweeney. Jean and Max Wasserman and my wife, Edys, took an active part in the Paris kinetic campaign, and I thank them for their indispensable and spirited support. Larry Rivers, a sometime kineticist and Tinguely collaborator, planted the seed of this exhibition's theme, and bears no responsibility for its final form.
I wish finally and especially to acknowledge the cooperation of the lenders whose generosity made the exhibition possible.

S. H.

Frontispiece. Tinguely: *Bascule 5,* 1965 (detail) (not in the exhibition).

Page 68. Schöffer: *Microtemps 11,* 1965 (detail) (cat. no. 30).

Nicolas Schöffer : *Lux 19*, 1959, brass with luminodynamic projections, Galerie Denise René, Paris

Two Kinetic Sculptors

"For me the machine is above all an instrument which permits me to be poetic."   *Jean Tinguely*

One of the aspects of modern existence that weighs most heavily on the artist's conscience but also significantly releases his imagination is the machine. The machine has in countless ways been a fertile source of inspiration for half a century. The Italian futurists seized on it to express their romantic enthusiasm for speed and dynamism; reacting violently to the mechanized mass destruction of the First World War, the Dadaists created their own version of an "infernal" machine in a variety of sardonic and fantastic inventions; Calder's mobiles later restored a spirit of optimism and innocent pleasure to the spectacle of mechanical forms in motion. Today ambivalent attitudes of high expectation and mistrust still surround the machine, and compete for attention in art. Mechanization stimulates in some artists millennial fantasies of a more perfect social organization and breeds in others a sense of helplessness and acute fears of dehumanization, fears which Charlie Chaplin's film burlesque, *Modern Times,* eloquently summarized many years ago.

In strictly formal terms, the machine has had a stunning and transforming impact on traditional modes of art and is responsible for the new category of motion or "kinetic" sculpture. A much wider range of expressive possibilities opened out to the artist when, in 1920, the Russian constructivist Naum Gabo for the first time made a sculpture that actually moved. Kinetic sculpture gained impetus in the thirties with Calder's invention of the air-driven mobile, so named by Marcel Duchamp whose "ready-made" bicycle wheel of 1913, mounted on a stool in a parody of the museum art object, was in fact the first motion sculpture of the century. The historical development of kinetic experiment includes many other important episodes: Man Ray's suspended coat-hangers, which anticipated Calder, Tatlin's Monument to the Third International, Gabo's *Vibrating Spring,* Moholy-Nagy's *Light Machine,* and the animated abstract films of Eggling and Richter.

The so-called "Movement Movement," a witty epithet coined by the film-maker Hans Richter, however, gained its real force as a group activity only in recent years, long after its pioneers, with the exception of Calder, had ceased to make significant advances. Perhaps the kinetic resur-

1

2

3

gence can be understood as a reaction to the emotionally stressed, highly individualistic painting and sculpture of the post-war period with its "crisis" mentality and mood of anxiety. Today one finds evidence on all sides that the pendulum in art has swung round to a more mechanical conception of creation, and renewed respect for collective discipline. Quite significantly, the new kinetic sculpture generally shuns private studio association and seems destined for public spaces as its ideal setting. It tries to meet the spectator on common ground through the use of standardized forms, and familiar industrial surfaces, even at the risk of some loss of personal intensity. However, this art movement, like so many others of the modern period, is far from uniform in tendency, and shows interesting contradictions.

Jean Tinguely and Nicolas Schöffer are two of the most original motion sculptors today; they take their stand at diverging and extreme esthetic positions based on impulsive freedom and science worship, expressive anarchy and strict intellectual plan. The Swiss Jean Tinguely fashions his kinetic structures in a studio outside of Paris with forms assembled from industrial scrap; his disarming, zestful art asserts qualities of vagabondage and a wild, picaresque individualism. Nicolas Schöffer, a Hungarian who like Tinguely has lived for many years in or around Paris, relates his altogether more calculated and meticulously engineered sculptures to idealistic social goals, and tries to harmonize the esthetic enterprise with our technological environment.

Humor, gusto, a taste for satire, and boundless energies of improvisation give Tinguely's sculptures their dual power as artistic inventions and clowning social commentary. His barn-studio in the village of Soisy-Sur-École looks like a wrecking yard, with its impossible spread and clutter of junked motors and machine parts, but from this unpromising and chaotic metal scrap miraculously emerge vivid forms that move, spin, clank and stutter into a surprising expressive and affective life. Tinguely's machines are really "anti-machine," as he has so often stated in print, aligned on the side of animal energy and vitalism. The hectic and uncertain life of his mechanical equipment, always on the verge of breakdown or disintegration, releases finally something pure like an arabesque of movement, or gesture, and each of his machines carries its own distinctive face and personality.

4   5   6

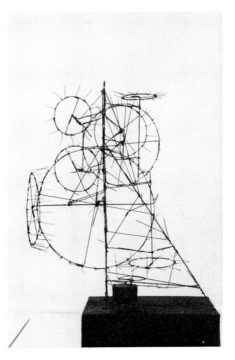

1. Tinguely at work on *Eureka*
   at the Lausanne Fair, Switzerland, 1964
   Photo by Monique Jacot

2. Marcel Duchamp : *Bicycle Wheel*, 1951
   Replica of lost original of 1913,
   51⅝ in. high, third version 1951
   Sidney Janis Gallery, New York

3. Paul Klee : *Twittering Machine*, 1922
   Watercolor, pen and ink, 16¼×12 in.
   The Museum of Modern Art, New York

4. Marcel Duchamp : *Coffee Mill*, 1911
   Oil on cardboard, 13×4⅞ in.
   Collection Mme. Maria Martins,
   Rio de Janeiro

5. Tinguely : *Prayer Wheel*, 1954 (cat. no. 41)
   Steel, motorized, 28 in. high
   Museum of Fine Arts, Houston

6. Tinguely : *Affair of the Heart*, 1963
   (cat. no. 64)
   Private collection, Seattle

He began to work in Paris twelve years ago as a conventional constructivist, but soon challenged the safer assumptions of his art, in a characteristic maneuver, by attaching to it and animating an ever more disreputable-looking assortment of machine rubbish. His work, indeed, for some time epitomized the new cult of junk, that sympathy evident in so much art of the late fifties for what is destitute, outlawed or banished to the trash heap in our prodigally wasteful society. In recent years his forms have become simpler and more monumental (he paints them black to give them solidity and perhaps gravity), with an altogether more sculptural effect. The manic cacophony of sound and motion that were his trademark are either absent, or reverberate only faintly in the background. He has proven himself a mature artist capable of growth and self-criticism, after rather sensational beginnings that seemed to promise only further outrages and assaults on conventional prejudice in the best theatrical tradition of debunking Dada. His greatest celebrity, and notoriety, came five years ago when he created in The Museum of Modern Art's garden a suicidal machine, entitled "Homage to New York," that annihilated itself with much sound and fury,

and set off a train of shocked or patronizing public reaction.

Nicolas Schöffer takes the engineer's optimistic view of the possibilities of a technological society, and works, in effect, for a more rational future. He tries to fit his art to the social circumstances of mechanical civilization. He is a devoted and proficient student of computer technology, and the intricate movements of his complex works are automatically programmed by electronic engineers under his close supervision. In 1954 in Paris, Schöffer made his first programmed sculpture, a machine-construction operating in three-dimensions with rotating reflecting disks, plastic screens and projectors which bathed them in a constantly changing colored light. He is also a visionary urban planner and designer whose fantastic solutions to our living problems may at first glance seem to exist in the realm of science fiction but become daily more plausible as the problems themselves call for increasingly imaginative and unprecedented solutions.

CYSP I is a typical Schöffer creation in a series whose title derives from the first letters of "cybernetics" and "spatiodynamics," words which the artist has given special

7

8

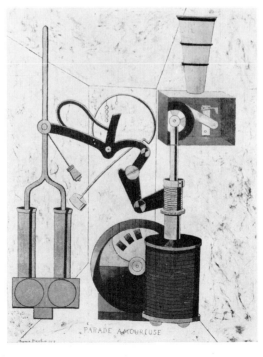

7. Tinguely with *Homage to New York* in the Museum of Modern Art Garden, New York, 1960
   Photo by David Gahr

8. Francis Picabia: *Amorous Procession*, 1917
   Oil on cardboard, 38¼ × 29⅛ in.
   Collection Mr. and Mrs. Morton G. Neumann, Chicago

personal meaning in his automated sculptures. The construction moves at different speeds in different directions, emits light and sound, creates color spectacle, and is electronically responsive to the human presence : certain colors and temperatures make it advance, others cause it to retreat. It is a robot work-of-art, an ingenious dual structure that stimulates and also chills the imagination, for like all purely mechanical spectacle—fireworks, moving colored lights, the play of illuminated fountains—it risks a certain inhumanity, no matter how ingenious or magical its mix of visual effects. Yet Schöffer has had the technical assurance and imaginative boldness to pursue the implications of his impersonal program on the grand scale, notwithstanding any possible Brave New World overtones of euphoric social conditioning : he recently designed for the city of Liège in Belgium a spectacular "cybernetic" tower 150 feet high which uses the glassed facade of a neighboring modern building, and the reflecting surface of the Meuse, as screens for moving light and color projections. In its season, the tower diverts the Liège population with regular performances. Few artists could conceive an esthetic work on such a monumental scale, or in so exposed and public a situation.

Schöffer's social conception of art is as enlightened and advanced as Tinguely's is egocentric. One artist creates with modern technology vast visual spectacles for popular consumption, and transforms the machine into an instrument of collective discipline. The other treats the machine ironically and even subversively, making it an agent of disorder and liberating forms of personal anarchy. Both views are valuable and constructive : Tinguely's inspired humor and irony in the face of the dilemmas posed by the machine age are no less comforting or persuasive than Schöffer's assurances that the technological environment can be mastered through art.

The promise of technology and its effrontery—its subversion of human instinct and identity—these are the conflicting emphases of the kinetic art of Schöffer and Tinguely. Both views of the machine are essential, however, if we want to see life whole and face the increasingly fantastic modern world of science and technology with some kind of serenity.

Sam Hunter   Director, The Jewish Museum

---

9. Tinguely : *Attila,* 1963 (cat. no. 67)
   Dwan Gallery, Los Angeles

10. Rube Goldberg : "Idea for keeping a buttonhole flower fresh"
    Collection Reuben Lucius Goldberg, New York

11. Tinguely : Sketch for *Rotozaza,* 1965 (cat. no. 102)
    Collection the artist

10

9

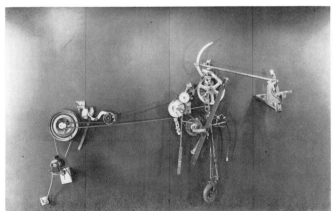

11

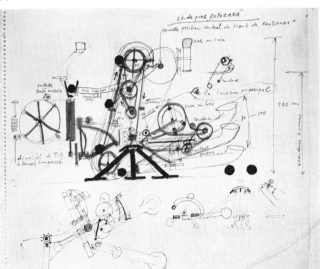

Jean Tinguely

Tinguely's form of mechanics is "meta-mechanics," which suggests an analogy with physics and metaphysics. Most of his early machines are machines that dance: gay, spirited, ironic, sometimes feverish. They are imaginative, inspiring and original in their movements, and they carelessly ignore the disciplines of the conventional machines of the world. From a machine one demands order and precision, reliability and regularity. Tinguely's point of departure is mechanical disorder. In his early works change and movement obeyed only the law of chance. He pitted the emancipated machine against the functional one, and conferred on his creations a glorious life of improvisation, happy inefficiency and shabbiness, expressing through his inspired inventions an indestructible freedom.

His sculptures of later years convey the meaninglessness of utilitarian mechanical function more ponderously and with sharper definition. The movements of his structures have become more deliberate and dramatic: their different parts are more clearly differentiated and personified. They seem condemned to a prisoner's life, always operating in the same place and repeating the same movements. As did Sisyphus, they strenuously lift a heavy weight which must inevitably be returned to its original position. The behavior and deportment of these sculptures possess a traumatic fatality. The sense of the absurdity of the mechanical environment which expressed itself comically in the past has now taken on sober and even tragic overtones. Also the movements of man, even his more intimate operations and performances would seem sometime to be parodied, held up to ridicule and at the same time made more monumental. One is reminded of the Berlin adage of the twenties, so Brechtian in spirit: "Müde, müde nichts wie müde, und so'n Ekel vor der Arbeit, und dann dieses lächerliche Geschlechtsleben." ("Weary, weary, always weary, and such disgust for work, and then this absurd sex life.")

Tinguely's works today express great pessimism regarding the machine's actual efficiency and worth. At the same time, however, they are basically optimistic with regard to the machine's irrational and religious potential. Indeed, his art radiates an optimism which is unusual in contemporary art, an optimism directed toward man, the creator of machines.

12. Robert Rauschenberg: *Empire II,* 1961
Mixed media, 61 × 29 × 58 in.
Leo Castelli Gallery, New York

13. Tinguely: *May Fair,* 1963 (cat. no. 68)
Dwan Gallery, Los Angeles

12

13

Machines carry and epitomize the mysteries of our time and technological environment. Everything in our surroundings is made or processed by machines, an unprecedented situation. We are compelled to see our lives as a function of the machine, and our vision has consequently become more mechanically oriented and less and less rooted in nature. The ubiquitous machine is often the creature and offspring of other machines. Machines give us prosperity but threaten us with their power and authority. Their capriciousness and their incorruptibility frighten and impress us. Can we master the machine today, or does it rule us? Is a machine less unique than a human being? Can one manufacture two identical machines? Is that not just as impossible as the notion of two identical men? What is, then, the difference between man and machine? When machines deceive us by ceasing to function according to our needs and desires, many of us are seized by surprise and despair. We stand astonished in the world of machines and yet are incapable of grasping whether or not we have allowed ourselves to be duped. Tinguely's art leads us to surmise that in the future man will be able to achieve another and more dignified relationship with the machine.

He also presents us with a considerable problem. Before his sculptures one must conclude that the transformation of a formal or psychological situation from one phase to another is neither interesting nor very important. The point of origin and the result are both of little consequence in the end because they are functions of change and bound to it. The decisive element in his work is metamorphosis and its manner of manifestation; indeed, the process of transformation, through motion, may be considered the only permanent condition of his work. Conversion from one state to another can be termed "good" or "bad" depending on whether we consider the result of the change an "improvement" or a "deterioration." Change in itself is neither good nor bad, since it remains outside such moral criteria. Fortunate is he who has arrived at a state in which he is able to love change for its own sake!

Two of the most surprising and influential concepts in art today are embodied in Tinguely's auto-creative and auto-destructive machines. One may justifiably compare his meta-matic drawing machines to Marcel Duchamp's ready-mades for richness of meanings, among others a

14

15

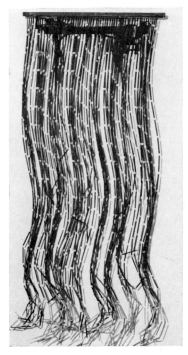

14. Man Ray: *Obstruction*, 1920
Replicas: 1944–1963
Reproduced courtesy the artist

15. Tinguely: *La Jalousie*, 1960 (cat. no. 54)
Collection Richard Lee Weisman, Beverly Hills

rather devastating critique of some of the automatic and ''informal'' art of the 1958 period, the date of Tinguely's invention. Any dissertation could only fail to exhaust the significance of his creation. The drawing machine adds another question mark after the question: Is art possible? Above all, it is a hallucinating vision of the position of art in the future.

The self-destroying machines throw an even more penetrating ray of light on our present cultural situation and the complexity of its thought. If art is a reflection of the fundamental ideas of a civilization, one can think of few more pertinent images or symbols. These machines have the richness and beauty of all very simple and therefore very great inventions. (What an appropriate name he gave to the first of these machines, ''Homage to New York,'' an homage to the capital of our modern mechanistic madness.)

When movement enters art, it demands that forms be definite. Movement returns them to the conditions and rhythms of life. Forms may take shape in a variety of materials, and they can be given infinite freedom in their motion patterns, but they must be able to work together harmoniously simply in order to move. It is in movement that we rediscover relationships and meanings which have so often been absent from much of today's art. Apollinaire may have envisaged the potential of kinetic art in 1913, when, writing about Marcel Duchamp, he declared that only an art which was free from all aesthetic considerations and used ''energy'' as a pictorial medium could hope to bring ''art and the people'' together. The fact that Tinguely's art object ''works'' freely opens a new line of communication between the artist and his audience. Tinguely, and Calder before him, dramatically cast the machine into the stagnant waters of modern art, and their energy has acted as a catalyst, producing a situation in which new events can take place.

If Tinguely were asked why he sometimes uses junk and scrap as elements in his sculptures, he would probably reply: ''Because they are so beautiful.'' Quite certainly he uses scrap for the same reason he works with motion. A piece of scrap has its unique form. One can either use it or discard it. It provides a goal, rejects aimlessness and embellishment, and stimulates the imagination.

In the large motion sculpture which Tinguely made in

16

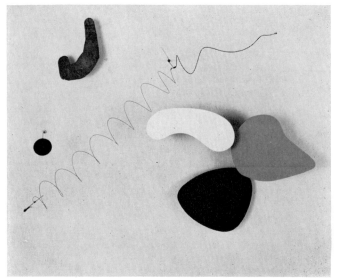

17

the fifties, bright color forms operated with quick, irregular jerky movements. The same form might repeat a gesture ten times consecutively, and then never repeat it again. Tinguely was playing on our sense of time in a way that makes us very patient with his work. His very directness and simplicity also persuade us to identify with his creations, and arouse enthusiastic feelings. He exploits time as a motive in art in the most fundamental and immediately comprehensible way, thus giving us a great appetite for similar explorations of our own.

With their unrepeatable and unique movements and sequences, Tinguely's machines exist in an enviable freedom. Their vitality, spontaneity, and lyricism bring to us ecstatic moments of life divorced entirely from moral precept or inhibition, from good and evil, right and wrong, beautiful or ugly. His machines are a piece of pure existence, eternally changeable, and they do not have to mean anything nor refer to anything. But one is mistaken to believe that their artistic message is innocent or harmless. They subvert the established order and convey a sense of anarchy and individual liberation which would otherwise not exist.

K. G. Hultèn   Director, Moderna Museet, Stockholm

18

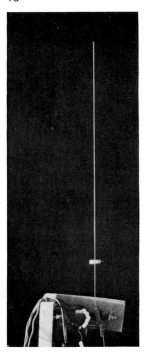

19

20

16. Alexander Calder: *The Orange Panel,* 1943
Wood, sheet metal, wire, motor, 36×48×7 in.
Collection Mrs. H. Gates Lloyd, Haverford, Penn.
Photo by P. E. Guerrero

17. Tinguely: *L'Oeuf D'Onocrotale 3,* 1958
(cat. no. 48)
Staempfli Gallery, New York

18. Naum Gabo: *Kinetic Construction:
Vibrating Spring,* 1920
Reproduced courtesy the artist

19. Naum Gabo: *Vibrating Spring* (in motion)
Reproduced courtesy the artist

20. Tinguely: *Constant 9,* 1960 (in motion)
(cat. no. 51)
Collection George W. Staempfli, New York

Nicolas Schöffer

Invention breeds invention, and an inventor can only invent, invent again, ceaselessly invent : he is in a universe of *perpetual invention.* But this mental universe he lives in, could it not be the real universe, that cosmos of which men form new concepts and new images commensurate with the progress of their knowledge, their experiments and techniques? The universe and the mind which ponders the universe are thus in a constant state of becoming. Neither one nor the other can stand still.

But undeniably, in this ever-unfolding story, this adventure without end, we can discern intervals. We can establish sign-posts, divide into periods, embrace wholes which we call civilizations. And from these civilizations we preserve precious and significant testimonies : masterpieces of art, particularly of the plastic arts, whenever they become available, in the form of static objects, for the examination, study, and delectation of the centuries. Of course some movement, some indecision, some infinity, a thousand secret and unpredictable treasures are hidden in these objects, are implicated, and this presence of movement, indecision, infinity, of all these marvelous, vital treasures, these

dynamic forces, can be sensed in works of art even though we know that they only exist artificially, through techniques which in no way contradict the static condition of the works in question, techniques which themselves partake of immobility : the processes of transposition, the stratagems of colored impasto and geometry which give the viewer of these rare, precious objects, fixed forever in their glory, the feeling that violent energies straining for release are being held captive in them.

But between periods of history there are crises and ruptures : man, or rather certain men in whom the collective conscience is more acute, sense that a civilization has had its say and reached its conclusion and that a new one is beginning to unfold its perspectives. New hypotheses from which flow new knowledge, also very real discoveries, verified, evident, a completely new view of the world and man's relation to it, prodigious changes in man's industry, his comforts, his behavior, his habits, all lead the creative imagination of those men of artistic bent to suddenly throw over all their old practices and dream up new forms and styles of the most delightful and shocking originality. This passionate desire to create the unheard-of, wasn't this the

21

21. Laszlo Moholy-Nagy : *Light Machine,* 1930
22. Schöffer : *Lux 2,* 1957 (cat. no. 8)
    Galerie Denise René, Paris

22

case, too, with the artists of that instant of crisis and revolution which separated the Middle Ages from the Renaissance? Their innocent cries of wonder and subversive daring still echo in our ears: *O tempora*! *Juvat vivere*! Or: *Che bella cosa questa prospettiva*! For a new world, the techniques of a new art, new arts themselves, integrally new.

Nicolas Schöffer, at this very moment when, in the same way, a new world is being born, has felt in the core of his artist's soul the fertile passion for universal change, from which springs the perpetually receptive state of his creative will. And it is with regard to the static quality of a work of art that this will asserts itself. From this moment motion becomes master of the work of art, without a backward glance, without regret, without remission. The logic of freedom is carried out inexorably.

Schöffer is by origin a painter and a sculptor, but these terms no longer are significant; and the demarcation between artist and engineer becomes obscured. Schöffer is that artist who must show himself to be in all things an engineer, that engineer who is in all things an artist. And beyond these distinctions he is an inventor. His function

is to invent and, as we said at the beginning of this little piece, such a function pursues its course without pause. For it is the movement of the universe which carries the inventor along, and that of human genius endlessly renewing the face of the universe.

Motion, then, communicates itself to images. Schöffer begins by inventing metal machines made from grills and skeletal frameworks combined with plates which project infinitely changing images onto a screen. Abstract images, or more exactly, arrangements. But these arrangements are constantly replaced one by another. To a quarter, to a hundredth of a second nearly, each of these arrangements is esthetically valid, that is, stable and perfect. But time sweeps them all away, not with the fluidity of music but in another sort of continuity, and, one might say, in a discontinuity extremely satisfying to the spirit of geometry. To plunge us into the realm of music, the impressionist realm, the intervention of color would be required, and very quickly Schöffer becomes preoccupied with color.

For his only concern must be the enrichment and broadening of his first experiments. These are to develop on an architectual and urbanistic scale. Since 1954 Schöffer has

23

24

23. Naum Gabo: Design for *Kinetic Construction*, 1922
Reproduced courtesty the artist

24. Schöffer exhibition at Le Musée des Arts Décoratifs, Paris, 1963, with *Spatiodynamic 22* in foreground

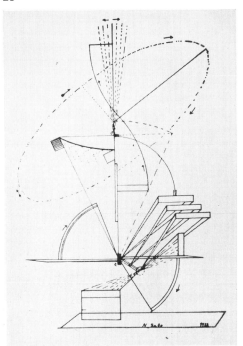

been building "spatiodynamic" towers which diffuse both music and images, entirely without outside intervention, made feasible through the use of electronics. From that invention to the creation of cybernetic machines was only a step, which the *prodigious magician* could not fail to take. On May 26, 1956, on the occasion of a "Night of Poetry" at the Sarah Bernhardt Theatre, he presented his first "cybernetic" sculpture, *CYSP I*, completed in collaboration with François Terny, an engineer of the Philips Company. It is a sensitive machine, endowed with an electronic brain, moving by itself, reacting to colors, to lights, to sounds, to silences. Let us listen to Guy Habasque, one of Schöffer's best exegetes, speak in praise of this astonishing creature: "The possibility of animating space in an entirely new way is coupled with the introduction of a temporal element which had never before entered into the concept of a work of art. Space and time are from now on indissolubly bound together. Furthermore, the work of art is no longer an inanimate object to be grasped at a glance, but constitutes in itself a veritable spectacle."

It is a spectacle and it participates in spectacles. It plays a part. It dances with living dancers. The ballet is certainly one of the arts which, until the present, has most closely approximated that "synthesis of the arts" which was the dream of so many fine talents of the most brilliant and celebrated periods of art, particularly at the close of the nineteenth century and during our own. It is even closer to that synthesis, achieves it more completely, when such component factors as the plastic arts, begin to animate themselves.

Even more extraordinary projects would come to mind, and our indefatigable demiurge was not able to stop there in the use of his magic wand. Ingenious modifications in the adjustment of his machines would permit him to make light and color give off a dazzling variety of effects. And a new birth, that of *Chronos I* in 1960, heralded a new art, yielder of new delights, "chronodynamism." For now it is to be time which patterns and modulates itself in these new works. This art is identified essentially with music and in it keys like those of the most glorious instruments are played upon to produce a flow of chromatic movements, of chromatic tempos, like that of a musical score, with a diversity and power of the same order, the diversity and power of a symphony—not to mention the fact that to these effects of

25

26

25. Schöffer and the Cybernetic Tower, Liege, Belgium, 1961
26. Electronic controls for the Liege Tower

color are added the most sumptuous effects of shadow, of light and of color intensity.

This chromatic activity, this structuring and staging of time identify a spatial event with a musical event. But beyond that, in addition to such splendors, they can also be accompanied by actual music, and the best composers of contemporary *musique concrète* collaborated with Schöffer. Everything is material for his genius, every element and every resource enter into the limitless possibilities of his constructions. In this sense, one of the latest of Schöffer's creations, a gigantic cybernetic tower at Liège, musically programmed with the cooperation of the composer Henri Pousseur, which projects its fantasies onto the glass facade of the Palace of Congress and, by night, the mirror of the waters of the Meuse, constitutes an achievement whose pageantry reaches the height of totality. Everything, indeed, even the most unpredictable forces of nature, of the city, the sky, the water, the night, all are used in it.

And so the conditions necessary to the art of long ago, to art as it has always been, are left behind by the creative energies which Nicolas Schöffer, artist of our century, sets free at will in response to the ever widening and more commanding scope of scientific invention. He expands the dominions of art. But, is this still art, will ask certain aggrieved souls who are loath to admit that at each new era in human history art has reaffirmed itself by changing its face, by making itself startling and unrecognizable. But it always was art. It always was, and still was, because it was *once more*—young, bold, alive with a fresher, stronger spirit. Such is the art of our age of dynamism and speed, of outdoing and integration, a *kinetic art.* It most certainly should give itself a new name, define itself distinctively, for its newness, like the new concept we have of the universe, should be signified. But this distinctiveness in no way alters the essence of art, which is always the same. This art of our times is in its essence eternal art, and merely follows after the arts of other eras which, when they first appeared, at the moment of their purest and most vivid self-assertion, in their *definition* of themselves, also seemed peculiar, startling, prodigious and animated by an imperious and insatiable ambition.

Jean Cassou

Formerly Chief Curator,
Le Musée de L'Art Moderne, Paris
Translated by Patsy Southgate

28

27. "Luminodynamic" performance of the Liege Tower
28. Cybernetic Tower, detail

27

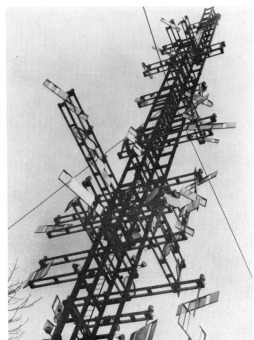

Non-Formalism

In the present phase of the evolution of artistic investigations, I believe that the work of art must be absolutely separated from the problem of form.

The formal aspect of works must be reduced to a minimum of signs that can create a visual (or audio-visual) language in the service of programmings of all kinds, diversified to their extreme limits, in order to realize temporal and microtemporal structures, organized with a view to obtaining amplitudes varied by the combined progress of the events (complex or simple), and their reciprocations.

The visual or audio-visual complex thus created can have deeper repercussions in the psychophenomenological field of the spectator, can take charge of him, so to speak, stimulate him or relax him, through aesthetic products that are all the more effective as they are non-formalist, and immaterial in their essence, in which durations replace volumes, and temporal rhythms replace the configurations of surfaces.

Programmed environments have the power of immediate communication.

Automation and electronic control give the work a versatility of adaptation hardly known until now ; the work becomes organic, rising to a level never before reached.

The work lives and adapts itself as much to the one who perceives it as the spectator lives and adapts himself to the environments created by the work, which are finally only extensions of himself transcended with a view to his own improvement.

These same considerations also affect the art of building on the larger scale of architecture, of city planning and land development.

Here as well, diversified yet simple and effective expressions will create structures from such elements as time, light, sound, environment and space.

The complex programming of these elements brings us to structured ensembles, where cybernetics can maintain an optimum equilibrium in a state of fluctuating permanence.

Nicolas Schöffer

29

30

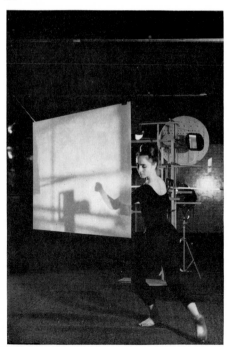

29 & 30. Ballet performances at the Schöffer exhibition, Le Musée des Arts Décoratifs, Paris, 1963

31. Schöffer at the keyboard of his *Musiscope*

32. *Musiscope* projection

33. Project for a light tower design on a University campus, the Paris suburbs, not executed

31

32

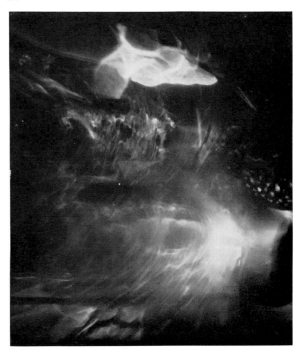

33

Nicolas Schöffer

Chronology

1912 Born in Kalocsa, Hungary. Studies at the Fine Arts Academy, Budapest.

1936 Moves to Paris and takes up studies at the École des Beaux-Arts. Has lived in Paris ever since.

1948 First one-man exhibition of paintings at Galerie Breteau, Paris. Develops "spatiodynamics" theories although still working in automatic and "informalist" painting manner.

1950 Exhibition of first kinetic sculpture at Galerie des Deux-Iles, Paris. Designs spatiodynamic electric clock with Henry Perlstein, an engineer.

1952 Exhibition, Galerie Mai, Paris.

1954 Constructs a sound-equipped spatiodynamic and cybernetic tower (for the Salon des Travaux Publics, Paris) with the technical assistance of Jacques Bureau, an engineer, in collaboration with the composer Pierre Henry.

1956 Designs house with invisible interior walls, formed by sharply differentiated temperature zones, at the Salon des Travaux Publics, Paris, in collaboration with the Philips and the Saint-Gobain Companies. Presents his first "cybernetic sculpture," *Cysp I*, at "Nuit de la Poésie" at the Sarah Bernhardt Theater, Paris. Maurice Béjart choreographs a ballet for *Cysp I* for the Festival of Avant-Garde Art in Marseille in Le Corbusier's Unité d'Habitation. *Cysp I* is shown also at "Cantate expérimentale" at the Academy of Fine Arts, Amsterdam.

1957 Presents experimental spatiodynamic spectacle, Evreux Theater, Paris. Develops "luminodynamics." Stages an experimental luminodynamic spectacle, Grand Central Station, New York City.

1958 Exhibition, Galerie Denise René, Paris.

1959 Shows two spatiodynamic sculptures in movement, with mobile projections in color, Musée de L'Art Moderne, Paris.

1960 Exhibition, Institute of Contemporary Arts, London. Develops "chronodynamics." Develops the *Musiscope* in collaboration with the engineer Julien Leroux.

1961 Exhibition, Palais des Beaux-Arts, Brussels. Presents the Musiscope at the Théâtre de France, Paris, with music by Pierre Jansen as part of the "Domaine Musical" concerts directed by Pierre Boulez. Designs and supervises construction of the "Spatiodynamic," or "Cybernetic" tower in La Boverie Park, Liège, Belgium. Tower is an abstract sculpture, 52 meters high, with 66 mirror plates, electronically controlled, which create audio-visual, "luminodynamic" spectacle, with musical accompaniment programmed by Henry Pousseur. Tower constructed by the Philips Company. Shows five moving sculptures with projections on two screens and peripheral projections at the VI Bienal, Sao Paolo, Brazil.

Broadcasts "luminodynamic variations" over French television in Paris in collaboration with J. Forestier and Jean Kerchbron.

1962 Presents the "Wall of Light" at the "Objet" exhibition, Musée des Arts Décoratifs, Paris, in collaboration with Christian van Lummel.

1963 Exhibition, Musée des Arts Decoratifs, Paris. Collaborates with Roger Planchon's Théâtre de la Cité in experimental presentation at Lyon-Villeurbane.

1964 Exhibition, Stedelijk Museum, Amsterdam, and Stedelijk van Abbemuseum, Eindhoven. Major representation at the exhibition, "Documenta III," Museum Fridericianum, Kassel, Germany. Included in "Painting and Sculpture of a Decade: 1954–64," Tate Gallery, London.

1965 First significant American presentation (7 sculptures), at the exhibition, "Kinetic and Optic Art Today," Albright-Knox Art Gallery, Buffalo, New York.

Jean Tinguely

Chronology

1925   Born in Fribourg, Switzerland.

1928   Family moves to Basel.

1939   Constructs sound-making "orchestra" out-of-doors by placing in a running brook some thirty water wheels each attached to a different object that makes noise.

1941   Attends Basel School of Fine Arts until 1945.

1945   Makes first constructions in wire, metal, wood and paper; "edible-sculpture" in grass.

1951   Moves to Paris where he has lived ever since.

1952   Develops mechanical scheme of "meta-matics" with asynchronous gears which permit the functional utilization of chance in kinetic constructions.

1954   First one-man exhibition, "Reliefs Métamécaniques," Galerie Arnaud, Paris. Included in exhibition, "Sculptures-Automobiles," Studio B24, Milan.

1955   Exhibition, Galerie Samlaren, Stockholm. Included in pioneering kinetic and optical abstraction exhibition, "Le Mouvement," Galerie Denise René, Paris. Shows "sound-making meta-robot painting-ma-chines." Participates in "Salon des Réalités Nouvelles," Paris. Included in "Eisenplastik" exhibition, Kunsthalle, Bern.

1956   Participates in the Festival of Avant-Garde Art in Marseille in Le Corbusier's Unité d'Habitation. Exhibition, Galerie Denise René, Paris.

1957   Exhibition, Galerie Denise René, Paris. Exhibition, Galerie Edouard Loeb, Paris.

1958   Exhibition, "Concert pour Sept Tableaux," Galerie Iris Clert, Paris. Exhibition, with Yves Klein, "Vitesse pure et stabilité monochrome," Galerie Iris Clert, Paris.

1959   Exhibition, Galerie Schmela, Düsseldorf. Flies over city and drops 150,000 manifestoes, "Für Statik." Exhibition, "Meta-matic," Galerie Iris Clert, Paris. Shows kinetic construction, "Meta-matic-automobile-odorante-et-sonore," at the first Biennale de Paris. It produces 40,000 multicolored paintings to be given away. Exhibition, Kaplan Gallery, London.

1960   First one-man exhibition in America, Staempfli Gallery, New York City. Creates "Homage to New York," a self-destroying machine, in the garden of The Museum of Modern Art, New York. Exhibiton, Galerie des Quatre Saisons, Paris. Shows machine that creates sculptures, and another that saws sculptures in half. Exhibition with Kricke and Luginbühl, Kunsthalle, Bern. Exhibition, Museum Haus Lange,

Krefeld. Shows machine designed "to destroy museums."

1961 Exhibition, Staempfli Gallery, New York City. Major representation in the international kinetic exhibition, "Rörelse I Konsten," at the Stedelijk Museum, Amsterdam; the Moderna Museet, Stockholm; the Louisiana Museum, Copenhagen (28 works shown). Participates in Paris "concert" with John Cage, Jasper Johns, Robert Rauschenberg, Niki de Saint-Phalle and David Tudor. Exhibition, Louisiana Museum, Copenhagen: first study for "The End of the World." Exhibition, Galerie Rive Droite, Paris. Exhibition, Galeria Schwarz, Milan.

1962 Exhibition, Galerie Handschin, Basel. Exhibition, Everett Ellin Gallery, Los Angeles. Exhibition, Alexander Iolas Gallery, New York City. Exhibition of Eleven Fountain-Sculptures, organized by Galerie Handschin, Kursaal, Basel. Participates in "The Construction of Boston," a theatrical event at the Maidman Theater, New York, written by Kenneth Koch with Robert Rauschenberg, Niki de Saint-Phalle and the Merce Cunningham dance company participating. Collaborates with the National Broadcasting Company in filming "The End of the World" in the Nevada desert. Organizes "Dylaby: Labyrinthe Dynamique" at the Stedelijk Museum, Amsterdam with Robert Rauschenberg, Martial Raysse, Niki de Saint-Phalle, Daniel Spoerri and Ultvedt. Shows *Narwa*, a "monster-machine," at the World's Fair, Seattle, Washington.

1963 Exhibition, Minami Gallery, Tokyo. Exhibition, Dwan Gallery, Los Angeles. Begins *Eureka*, a giant machine (30 feet high, 15 feet wide, 22 feet long), for the National Swiss Exhibition at Lausanne, commissioned by the Swiss government. Completed in 1964, the machine still stands on the fair grounds.

1964 Exhibition, Galerie Alexandre Iolas, Geneva. Exhibition, Kunsthalle, Baden-Baden. Exhibition, Zwirner Gallery, Cologne. Included in "Documenta III," Museum Fridericianum, Kassel, Germany. Included in "Painting and Sculpture of a Decade: 1954–64," the Tate Gallery, London. Exhibition, Galerie Alexandre Iolas, Paris. The entire exhibition is acquired by the Museum of Fine Arts, Houston, Texas. Included in "Mouvement 2," Galerie Denise René, Paris.

1965 Exhibition, Alexander Iolas Gallery, New York City, in collaboration with the Dwan Gallery, Los Angeles. Included in "Kinetic and Optic Art Today," Albright-Knox Art Gallery, Buffalo, New York. Exhibition, the Museum of Fine Arts, Houston, Texas. "Trois Sculpteurs: César, Roël D'Haese, Tinguely," shown at the Musée des Arts Décoratifs, Paris. Major representation at the VIII Bienal, Sao Paolo, Brazil, under Swiss auspices. Tinguely awarded minor prize for "experimental sculpture" which he refused to accept, however. Included in "Lumière et Mouvement" exhibition, Kunsthalle, Bern.

Unless otherwise noted, the dimensions are given in inches, height preceding width. Where three dimensions are noted, their order is height, depth and length.

*Illustrated.

Nicolas Schöffer

Sculpture

1* **Spatiodynamic Relief 2,** 1950
Aluminum and plexiglass, motorized, 66⅞×25⅝
Galerie Denise René, Paris

2* **Spatiodynamic Relief 4,** 1950
Aluminum and plexiglass, 39⅜×19⅜
Galerie Denise René, Paris

3* **Spatiodynamic 17,** 1953
Steel, motorized, 55⅛×47¼
Galerie Denise René, Paris

4 **Spatiodynamic 19,** 1953
Brass, steel and aluminum, motorized, 39⅞×30½
Jane Wade Ltd., New York

5* **Spatiodynamic 20,** 1953
Brass, motorized, 22⅞×18⅞
Galerie Denise René, Paris

6* **Spatiodynamic 22,** 1954
Cast steel and aluminum, 49½×29¼×22¾
Albright-Knox Gallery, Buffalo

7* **Cysp 1,** 1956
Steel and aluminum, motorized, 70⅞×63
Galerie Denise René, Paris

8* **Lux 2,** 1957
Steel, aluminum and plastic with luminodynamic projections, motorized, 65×70⅞
Galerie Denise René, Paris

9 **Lux 19,** 1959
Brass and copper, motorized, 39⅜×20½
Galerie Denise René, Paris

10* **Chronos 3,** 1959 (model for Cybernetic Tower, Liège, Belgium)
Duraluminum, 14 feet 9⅜×17½ inches
Galerie Denise René, Paris

11* **Musiscope,** 1960
Visual organ with plastic screen for color projections, 78¾×78¾
Galerie Denise René, Paris

12* **Serial Relief 1,** 1962
Steel and cadmium nickel, 25¾×17¼
Galerie Denise René, Paris

13* **Serial Relief 2,** 1962
Steel and cadmium nickel, 26×17½
Galerie Denise René, Paris

14 **Serial Relief 3,** 1962
Steel, brass and copper, 17⅛×11¾
Galerie Denise René, Paris

15 **Serial Relief 4,** 1962
Steel, brass and copper, 17⅛×11¾
Galerie Denise René, Paris

16* **Chronos 5,** 1962
Duraluminum, motorized, 78¾×60
Galerie Denise René, Paris

17* **Serial Relief 1,** 1963
Plexiglass, 15⅜×9¼
Galerie Denise René, Paris

18 **Serial Relief 2,** 1963
Plexiglass, 9¼×15⅜
Galerie Denise René, Paris

19 **Serial Relief 3,** 1963
Plexiglass, 9¼×15⅜
Galerie Denise René, Paris

20 **Serial Relief 4,** 1963
Plexiglass, 9¼×15⅜
Galerie Denise René, Paris

21 **Serial Relief 5,** 1963
Plexiglass, 9¼×15⅜
Galerie Denise René, Paris

22 **Serial Relief 6,** 1963
Plexiglass, 9¼×15⅜
Galerie Denise René, Paris

23 **Serial Relief 7,** 1963
Plexiglass, 9¼×15⅜
Galerie Denise René, Paris

24 **Serial Relief 8,** 1963
Plexiglass, 9¼×15⅜
Galerie Denise René, Paris

25 **Serial Relief 9,** 1963
Plexiglass, 9¼×15⅜
Galerie Denise René, Paris

26 **Serial Relief 10,** 1963
Plexiglass, 9¼×15⅜
Galerie Denise René, Paris

27 **Microtemps 4,** 1963
Steel, duraluminum and plexiglass, motorized, 37⅜×20⅞
Galerie Denise René, Paris

28 **Microtemps 5,** 1963
Steel, duraluminum and plexiglass, motorized, 37⅜×20⅞
Galerie Denise René, Paris

29* **Chronos 6,** 1964
Steel, duraluminum and plexiglass,
   motorized, 66⅞×65⅝
Galerie Denise René, Paris

30* **Microtemps 11,** 1965
Steel, duraluminum and plexiglass,
   motorized, 35⅜×24
Galerie Denise René, Paris

31* **Microtemps 12,** 1965
Steel, duraluminum and plexiglass,
   motorized, 35⅜×24
Galerie Denise René, Paris

Photograph Enlargements

32 The Cybernetic City: spatiodynamic theater

33 The Cybernetic City: residential quarter

34 The Cybernetic City: scientific research center

35 The Cybernetic City: administrative center

36 The Cybernetic City: cultural center

37 Luminodynamic spectacle

38* Design for a university campus

39 Cybernetic Tower, La Boverie Park, Liège, Belgium

40 A performance of the Liège Cybernetic Tower

Jean Tinguely

Sculpture

41* **Prayer Wheel,** 1954
Steel, motorized, 27½ high
Museum of Fine Arts, Houston
(Shown at The Jewish Museum only)

42 **Meta-Malevich,** 1954
Painted steel, motorized, 24×20
Museum of Fine Arts, Houston
(Shown at The Jewish Museum only)

43* **Polychrome Meta-Mechanic,** 1954
Painted steel, motorized, 46 high
Collection Mr. and Mrs. Max Wasserman, Chestnut Hill
(Shown at The Jewish Museum only)

44 **Concert for 7 Constructions,** 1955–58
Mixed media, motorized, each panel approx. 19×19
Collection the artist

45* **Polychrome Relief,** 1955
Painted steel, motorized, 16½×59
Museum of Fine Arts, Houston
(Shown at The Jewish Museum only)

46 **Meta-Mechanic Relief,** 1955
Mixed media, motorized,
   33½×19⅝ inches × 11 feet 2 inches
Moderna Museet, Stockholm

47 **Meta-Kandinsky,** 1955
Painted steel, motorized, 54½×16½×15¾
Dwan Gallery, Los Angeles

48* **L'Oeuf D'Onocrotale 3,** 1958
Painted steel, motorized, 36×33½
Staempfli Gallery, New York

49 **Meta-Matic 10,** 1959
Painted steel and paper, motorized, 25×18×36
Collection the artist

50 **Puss in Boots,** 1959
Painted steel and wire, motorized, 30⅛ high
The Museum of Modern Art, New York, Philip C. Johnson Fund
(Shown at The Jewish Museum only)

51* **Constant 9,** 1960
Painted steel and wood, motorized, 13½ high
Staempfli Gallery, New York

52 **La Cloche,** 1960
Mixed media, motorized, 41×17×74
Dwan Gallery, Los Angeles

53 **Tricycle,** 1960
Metal scrap, 59 high with base
Staempfli Gallery, New York

54* **La Jalousie,** 1960
Mixed media, motorized, 87×14×36
Collection Richard Lee Weisman, Beverly Hills

55* **IBM,** 1960
Mixed media, 10½ high
Collection George W. Staempfli, New York

56 **La Sorcière,** 1960
Mixed media, motorized, 63×20×22
Dwan Gallery, Los Angeles

57 **Radio Cocktail,** 1961
Mixed media, with feather, motorized, 21 high
Collection Mr. and Mrs. Max Wasserman, Chestnut Hill

58* **Baluba II,** 1961
Mixed media, motorized, 56 high
Collection of Mr. and Mrs. Robert B. Mayer, Winnetka
(Shown at The Jewish Museum only)

59 **Radio Plastic,** 1962
Plexiglass and radio parts, 35×36
Alexander Iolas Gallery, New York

60 **WNYR Radio Relief,** 1962
Steel, machine parts mounted on wood, motorized, 23×32
Dwan Gallery, New York

61* **Radio,** 1962
Metal scrap and radio parts, 30 high
Alexander Iolas Gallery, New York

62 **Viridiana,** 1963
Steel, motorized, 31½×24
The William N. Copley Collection, New York
(Shown at The Jewish Museum only)

63 * **Hannibal,** 1963
Painted steel and metal scrap, motorized, 46×40×108
Collection Robert Rauschenberg, New York

64 * **Affair of the Heart,** 1963
Steel, motorized, 35×13
Private Collection, Seattle

65 * **Samurai,** 1963
Painted steel, motorized, 74×25
Dwan Gallery, New York

66 **Odessa,** 1963
Painted steel, motorized, 51×31
Collection Virginia Dwan, New York

67 * **Attila,** 1963
Steel, machine parts mounted on wood, motorized,
    10 feet 6 inches × 24 inches × 16 feet
Dwan Gallery, Los Angeles

68 * **May Fair,** 1963
Metal scrap and machine parts, motorized, 42×28×62
Dwan Gallery, Los Angeles

69 **M.K. III,** 1964
Painted steel, motorized, 36¼×82½
Museum of Fine Arts, Houston
(Shown at The Jewish Museum only)

70 * **Clarissa,** 1964
Painted steel, motorized, 64×52
Alexander Iolas Gallery, New York

71 **Sisyphus,** 1964
Painted steel, motorized, 88×30
Alexander Iolas Gallery, New York

72 **Iwo Jima,** 1965
Painted steel, motorized, 28¾×29¼
Collection John G. Powers, Hackensack

73 **Pop, Hop and Op & Co.,** 1965
Painted steel, motorized, 43¼×82⅝
Alexander Iolas Gallery, New York

74 * **Isidor,** 1965
Painted steel, motorized, 88⅝×19⅝
Collection Mr. and Mrs. Max Wasserman, Chestnut Hill

75 * **Motor Cocktail,** 1965
Painted steel, motorized, 27 high
Alexander Iolas Gallery, New York

76 **Celestin,** 1965
Painted steel, motorized, 88×30
Alexander Iolas Gallery, New York

77 **Southampton 3,** 1965
Painted steel, motorized, 26 high
Collection Mr. and Mrs. Larry Rivers, New York

78 **Dissecting Machine,** 1965
Painted steel, mannikins, saws, motorized, 73×74×84
Collection the artist

79 **The Horse,** 1965
Painted steel with rocking horse head, motorized, 25 high
Collection the artist

Drawings

80 Drawing executed in collaboration with
    Meta-Matic 4, 1960
Ink on paper, 18×16
Staempfli Gallery, New York

81 Drawing executed in collaboration with
    Meta-Matic 4, 1960
Ink on paper, 18×16
Staempfli Gallery, New York

82 Sheet of 4 sketches for **Homage to New York,** 1960
Ink and pencil on paper, 16×18
Staempfli Gallery, New York

83 Sketch for **Homage to New York,** 1960
Felt pen and ink on bristol board, 22⅛×28
The Museum of Modern Art, New York, Gift of Peter Selz

84 "Corrected" design for a moving "do-it-yourself"
    sculpture by Jean Tinguely, 1962
Pencil on mechanical reproduction, 24×37
Collection Mr. and Mrs. Phillip A. Bruno, New York

85 Sketches for **Ivan, L'Espoir** and **La Sorcière,** 1963
Ink on paper, 9×12
Dwan Gallery, Los Angeles

86 Sketch for **La Cloche,** 1963
Ink on paper, 9×12
Dwan Gallery, Los Angeles

87 Sketch for **Totem 2** and **La Jalousie,** 1963
Ink on paper, 9×12
Dwan Gallery, Los Angeles

88 Sketch for **Eureka,** 1963
Pencil on paper, 10¾×14½
Alexander Iolas Gallery, New York

89 * Sketch for **Eureka,** 1963
Ink on paper, 8½×11⅝
Alexander Iolas Gallery, New York

90 Untitled drawing, 1963
Pencil on paper, 9¾×14
Dwan Gallery, Los Angeles

91 **Christmas Letter,** 1964
Collage and ink on paper, 14⅝×20½
Collection George W. Staempfli, New York

92 Untitled, 1964
Ink on paper, 14⅛×19½
(Stamp of Auberge du Cheval-Blanc, Egyptian
    figure playing instrument, forks, birds)
Alexander Iolas Gallery, New York

93 Untitled, 1964
Collage and ink on paper, 19½×14⅛
(Arrow and airplane at left,
   girl scattering seed above signature)
Alexander Iolas Gallery, New York

94 Untitled, 1964
Collage and ink on paper, 14½×10¾
(Arrow and printed legend,
   "Any Advance," at lower right)
Alexander Iolas Gallery, New York

95 Untitled, 1964
Collage and ink on paper, 12⅜×10½
(Number "66" and "Napoli" at center)
Alexander Iolas Gallery, New York

96* Untitled, 1965
Collage and ink on paper, 17¼×15¾
("1982" at bottom center)
Alexander Iolas Gallery, New York

97 Sketch for **Rotozaza,** 1965
Ink on paper, 12⅝×16⅛
(Smaller insert drawing dated "28. VII. 65,"
   pasted at upper left)
Collection the artist

98 Sketch for **Rotozaza,** 1965
Ink on paper, 12⅝×16⅛
(Legend at bottom of sheet,
   "this is 'ROTAZAZA' alias 'MATER' . . .")
Private Collection, New York

99 Sketch for **Halloween,** 1965
Pencil on paper, 13⅞×17
Alexander Iolas Gallery, New York

100 Sketch for **Bascule,** 1965
Pencil and ink on paper, 13⅞×17
Alexander Iolas Gallery, New York

101 Sketch for **Bascule,** 1965
Pencil on paper, 13⅞×17
Alexander Iolas Gallery, New York

102* Sketch for **Rotozaza,** 1965
Ink and water color on paper, 15×18
(Top right, "Etude pour Rotozaza")
Collection the artist

Sculpture Addenda

Eos 7, 1965
Steel, motorized, 78×37×60
Collection the artist

Eos B, 1965
Steel, motorized, 10×3×9 feet
Collection the artist

Schöffer: *Spatiodynamic Relief 2,* 1950 (cat. no. 1), Galerie Denise René, Paris

Schöffer: *Spatiodynamic Relief 4,* 1950 (cat. no. 2), Galerie Denise René, Paris

Schöffer: *Serial Relief,* 1963 (not in exhibition) Plexiglass, 17⅛×11¾, Galerie Denise René, Paris

Schöffer: *Serial Relief,* 1962 (not in exhibition)
Steel and cadmium nickel, 26×17½
Galerie Denise René, Paris

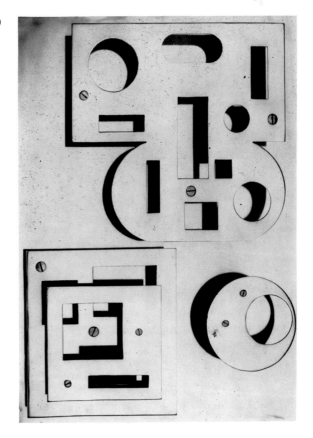

Schöffer: *Serial Relief 2,* 1962 (cat. no. 14)
Galerie Denise René, Paris

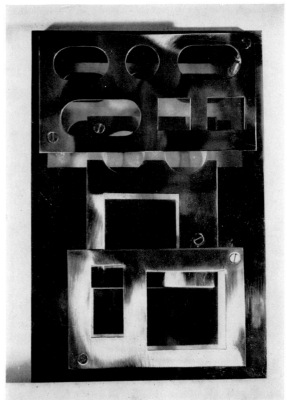

Schöffer: *Spatiodynamic 22,* 1954 (cat. no. 6), Albright-Knox Art Gallery, Buffalo

Schöffer: *Spatiodynamic 20,* 1953 (cat. no. 5), Galerie Denise René, Paris

Schöffer: *Spatiodynamic 17,* 1953 (cat. no. 3), Galerie Denise René, Paris

Spatiodynamic 17 (in motion)

Cysp I, 1956 (cat. no. 7), Galerie Denise René, Paris

Schöffer: *Chronos 5,* 1962 (cat. no. 16), Galerie Denise René, Paris

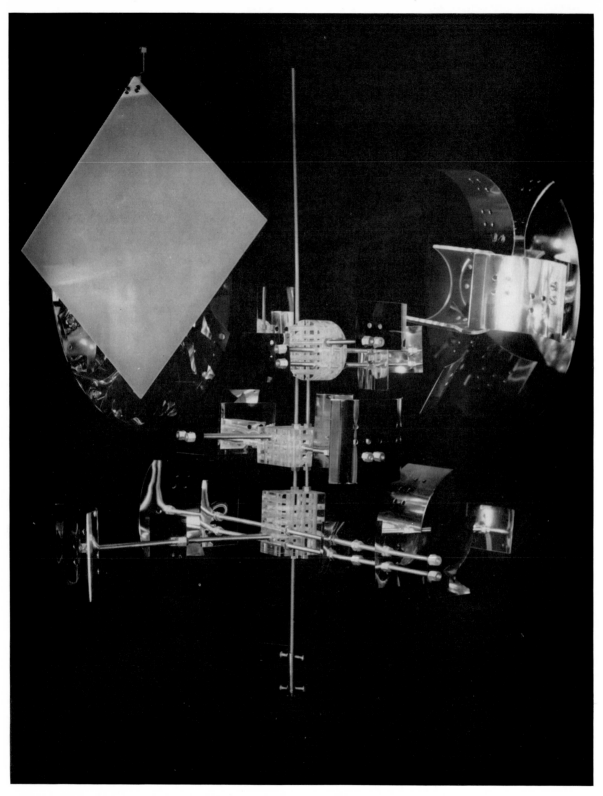

Schöffer: *Microtemps 11,* 1965 (cat. no. 30), Galerie Denise René, Paris

Schöffer: *Microtemps 11* (in motion)

Schöffer: *Microtemps 11* (in motion)

Schöffer : *Microtemps 12,* 1965 (detail, in motion, cat. no. 31), Galerie Denise René, Paris

Schöffer: *Chronos 6,* 1964 (cat. no. 29), Galerie Denise René, Paris

Schöffer: *Chronos 3* (detail), 1959 (cat. no. 10), Model for the Liège Cybernetic Tower, Galerie Denise René, Paris

Project for the Cybernetic City, university center, 36,000 feet in height, designed to house 30,000 students

Free drawing of the Cybernetic City

Tinguely: *Polychrome Meta-Mechanic,* 1954 (cat. no. 43), Collection Mr. and Mrs. Max Wasserman, Chestnut Hill

Tinguely: *Polychrome Relief,* 1955 (cat. no. 45), Museum of Fine Arts, Houston

Tinguely: *Meta-Matic No. 9*, 1959, mixed media, motorized, 35½ in. high (not in exhibition)

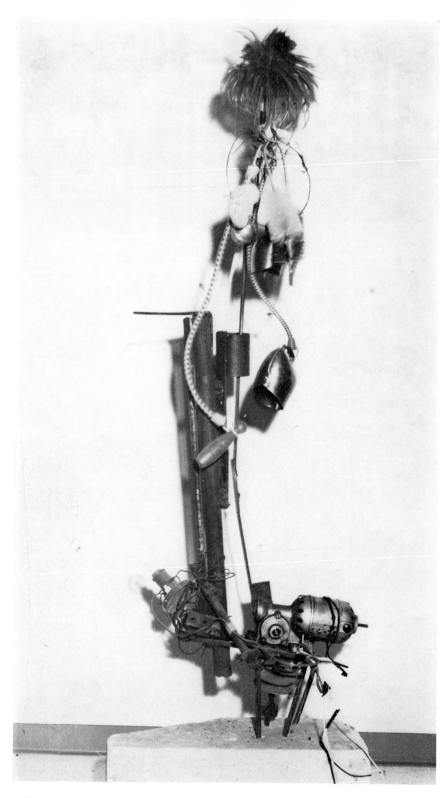

Tinguely: *Baluba II,* 1961 (cat. no. 58),
Collection Mr. and Mrs. Robert B. Mayer, Winnetka

Tinguely : *Furs,* 1962, mixed media, motorized, 45¼ in.
Museum of Fine Arts, Houston (not in exhibition)

Tinguely: *Radio,* 1962 (cat. no. 61)
Alexander Iolas Gallery, New York

Tinguely: *I.B.M.,* 1960 (cat. no. 55), Collection George W. Staempfli, New York

Tinguely : *M.K. III,* 1964 (cat. no. 69), Museum of Fine Arts, Houston

M.K. III, 1964 (in motion)

Tinguely : *Samural,* 1963 (cat. no. 65), Dwan Gallery, New York

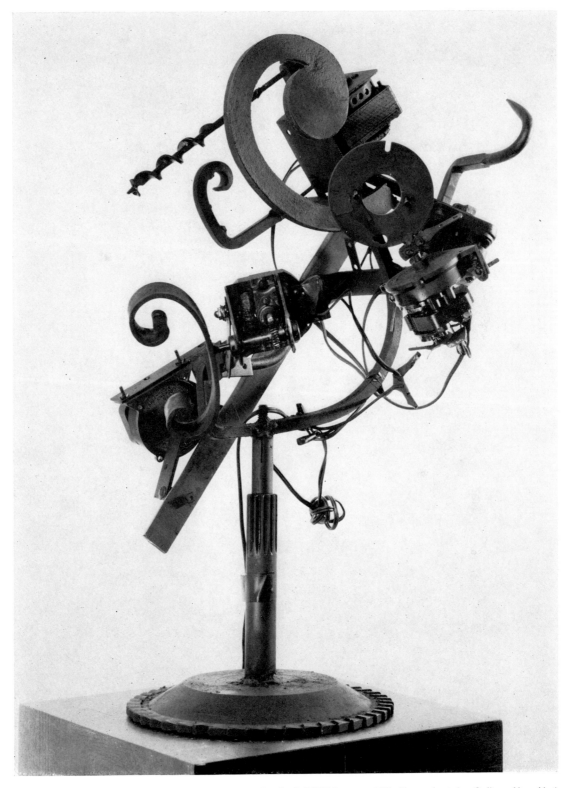

Tinguely: *Motor Cocktail,* 1965 (cat. no. 75), Alexander Iolas Gallery, New York

Tinguely: *Eureka,* 1964, motorized construction, 30 feet high
Official symbol and signal tower of the Lausanne National Fair, Switzerland

Tinguely: *Drawing for "Eureka,"* 1964 (cat. no. 89)
Alexander Iolas Gallery, New York

Tinguely : *Clarissa,* 1964 (cat. no. 70)
Alexander Iolas Gallery, New York

Tinguely : *Untitled,* 1965 (cat. no. 96), Alexander Iolas Gallery, New York

Tinguely: *Isidor,* 1965 (cat. no. 74), Collection Mr. and Mrs. Max Wasserman, Chestnut Hill

Tinguely: *Pop, Hop* and *Op* & *Co.,* 1965 (cat. no. 73), Alexander Iolas Gallery, New York

Tinguely: *Le Char,* 1965, painted steel, motorized, 88 in. × 64 in. × 16 ft. 8 in., Alexander Iolas Gallery, New York (not in exhibition)

Detail of *Le Char* (in motion)

Selected Bibliography

Nicolas Schöffer

Books

Habasque, Guy and Ménétrier, Jacques, *Nicolas Schöffer.* Editions du Griffon, Neuchâtel, Switzerland, 1963. Introduction by Jean Cassou, with a phonograph record, "Spatiodynamism," music by Pierre Henry, produced by "La Diffusion magnétique sonore."

Seuphor, Michel, *The Sculpture of this Century.* George Braziller, New York, 1959.

Exhibition Catalogues

Paris, Galerie des Deux-Iles (Exhibition), 1950. Preface by Raymond Bayer.

Paris, Galerie Mai (Exhibition), 1952. Preface by Michel Seuphor.

Paris, Galerie Denise René (Exhibition), 1958. Preface by Marcel Brion.

London, Institute of Contemporary Arts (Exhibition), 1960. Prefaces by Jean Cassou and Guy Habasque.

Brussels, Palais des Beaux-Arts (Exhibition), 1961. Prefaces by Jean Cassou and Jean Seaux.

Paris, Musée des Arts Décoratifs (Nicolas Schöffer), 1963. Preface by Michel Faré with essay by Guy Habasque.

Amsterdam, Stedelijk Museum (Nicholas Schöffer), 1964. Also shown at Eindhoven, Stedelijk van Abbemuseum. Preface by Jean Cassou with essay by Guy Habasque.

Kassel, Museum Fridericianum (Documenta III), 1964.

London, Tate Gallery (Painting and Sculpture of a Decade, 1954–1964), 1964.

Buffalo, New York, Albright-Knox Art Gallery (Kinetic and Optic Art Today), 1965.

Articles by the Artist

"L'artiste et la société—La socialisation du rôle de l'artiste." In collaboration with Dr. Vinchon. *Aujourd 'hui,* No. 10, November, 1956.

"Arts et Sciences." In collaboration with Guy Habasque, *Aujourd 'hui,* No. 1–14, 1955–1957.

"Essai d'analyse de l'évolution des tendances dans l'art d'après-guerre." In collaboration with Dr. Sivadon. *Aujourd 'hui,* No. 8, June, 1956.

"Integration de l'architecture dans la sculpture." *Architecture d'Aujourd 'hui,* 34 :105–7. June, 1964.

"Notes on a new trend: multi-dimensional animated works." Translated by M. Tobin and Guy Habasque. *Yale French Studies,* nos. 19–20 :36–9. 1957–1958.

"Structure et Indétermination, Formes Ouvertes, Anamorphose Optique et Temporelle." *Art International,* v. V /5–6 :90–91. June–August, 1961.

Articles

Apollo, "Schöffer at the Galerie Denise René," v. 69 :47. February, 1959.

Arts (Paris), "Des peintures à la Galerie Breteau," p. 5. April 2, 1948.

Ashton, Dore, "Way Beyond." *Arts and Architecture,* v. 72 :34–5. August, 1955.

Bordier, Roger, "L'art et la manière. Sonia Delaunay.... Schöffer." *Art d'Aujourd 'hui,* ser. 5, no. 6 :12–17. September, 1954.

Brunais, Jean, "Théâtre spatiodynamique." *Science et Vie.* No. 469, October, 1956.

Cassou, Jean, "Schöffer." *Art International,* v. V /5–6 :86–89. June–August, 1961. Reprint of preface to exhibition at Institute of Contemporary Arts, London, 1960.

Charbonnier, Georges. "Nicolas Schöffer." *Connaissance des Arts,* No. 108, February, 1961.

Emert, John, "Nicolas Schöffer." *Architectural Design,* No. 12, December, 1960.

Fitzsimmons, James, "Nicolas Schöffer." *Arts and Architecture,* v. 71, No. 4, April, 1954.

Habasque, Guy, "Nicolas Schöffer et le spatiodynamisme." *Aujourd 'hui,* 1st yr., no. 3 :26–27. May-June, 1955.

Habasque, Guy, "Peinture mobile." *Aujourd 'hui art et architecture,* 2nd yr., no. 12 :31. April, 1957.

Habasque, Guy, "Conversation dans l'atelier : Schöffer." *L'Oeil,* no. 81 :42–7+. September, 1961.

Habasque, Guy, "Art et technique : la cinétique." *XXe Siècle,* no. 23 :88. December, 1961.

International Lighting Review, "The Luminoscope and its Possibilities," v. 10, No. 5, 1959.

Legrand, F. C., "Neue peinture et la sculpture au défi." *Quadrum,* no. 7 :37+. 1959.

Lévêque, Jean-Jacques, "Nicolas Schöffer : Premier Spectacle Audio-visual au Salon de l'Automobile." *Arts* (Paris), no. 885 :11. October 10–16, 1962.

Menetrier, Jacques, "Les spectacles de Nicolas Schöffer." *Planète,* No. 4. 1962.

L'Oeil, "Confrontation internationale : la deuxième exposition Documenta organisée au Museum Fridericianum de Kassel," no. 57 :27. September, 1959.

L'Oeil, "Sculpture temporelle," no. 69 :52. September, 1960.

Popper, F., "Movement and light in today's art." *Arts and Architecture,* v. 81 :24–5+. April, 1964.

Ragon, Michel, "Schöffer révèle sa ville idéale." *Arts* (Paris), no. 936 :10. November 13–19, 1963.

Richter, H., "Exposition du mouvement à Amsterdam." *Aujourd 'hui,* v. 5-54–5. May, 1961.

Schneider, Pierre, "Art news from Paris." *Art News,* v. 62 :49. January, 1964.

Time Magazine, "Spatiodynamism," v. 66, no. 4, July, 1955.

Verken, Monique. "Le Sculpteur Nicolas Schöffer. Formes et Lumières." *Beaux Arts,* no. 940 :8–9. June, 1961.

Wescher, Herta, "Schöffer." *Cimaise,* ser. 2, no. 2 :11–12. November–December, 1954.

Wretholm, Eugen, "Nicolas Schöffer's spatiodynamism." *Konstrevy,* v. 36, no. 2 :72–75. 1960.

Films

Sculptures en mouvement et projections. 1956. Color short made in collaboration with Jacques Brissot.

Spatiodynamisme. 1957. Color short made with Tinto Bras.

Mayola. 1958. Color short made with Henry Gruel, E. Timmer, music by T. Dissevelt.

Ten minute sequence in color, for the film *Le propre de L'homme* by Claude LeLouche. 1960.

Jean Tinguely

Books

Maillard, Robert, ed., *Dictionary of Modern Sculpture.* Tudor Publishing Co., New York, 1960. Entry on Tinguely written by Michel Conil-Lacoste.

Seuphor, Michel, *The Sculpture of this Century.* George Braziller, Inc., New York, 1959.

Tomkins, Calvin, *The Bride and the Bachelors,* The Viking Press, New York, 1965.

Exhibition Catalogues

Paris, Galerie Arnaud (Reliefs Meta-mecanique), 1954. Preface by R. van Gindertael.

Paris, Galerie Denise René (le Mouvement), 1955. Tinguely included in pioneering exhibition of the kinetic and optical abstraction with Agam, Bury, Calder, Duchamp, Soto, Vasarely. Statements for catalogue by R. Bordier, K. G. Hultèn, V. Vasarely.

Dusseldorf, Galerie Schmela, 1958. Foreword by Pierre Restany.

Bern, Kunsthalle (Kricke, Bernhard, Luginbühl, Jean Tinguely), 1960. Introduction by Franz Meyer.

Krefeld, Museum Haus Lange (Jean Tinguely), 1960. Introduction by Paul Wember.

New York, Museum of Modern Art (Homage to New York), 1960. One-leaf broadsheet with statements, by Dore Ashton, Alfred H. Barr, Jr., Marcel Duchamp, Richard Huelsenbeck, K. G. Hultèn and Peter Selz.

New York, Staempfli Gallery, 1960.

New York, Staempfli Gallery, 1961.

Stockholm, Moderna Museet (Rörelse I. Konsten), 1961. Foreword by K. G. Hultèn and "Garden Party" by J. W. Kluver (later reprinted by *Zero*).

Amsterdam, Stedelijkmuseum (Dylaby: Labyrinthe Dynamique), 1962.

Basel, Galerie Handschin, 1962.

New York, Alexander Iolas Gallery, in collaboration with Dwan Gallery, Los Angeles, 1962. Poem by W. H. B. Sandberg.

Tokyo, Minami Gallery (Tinguely), 1963. Foreword by Yoshiaki Tono.

Baden-Baden, Kunsthalle (Jean Tinguely), 1964. Statements by Dietrich Mahlow and Godula Buchholz.

Kassel, Museum Fridericianum (Documenta III), 1964.

London, Tate Gallery (Painting and Sculpture of a Decade, 1954–64), 1964.

Buffalo, New York, Albright-Knox Art Gallery (Kinetic and Optic Art Today), 1965.

Houston, Texas, The Museum of Fine Arts (Jean Tinguely Sculptures), 1965. Introduction by James Johnson Sweeney.

New York, Alexander Iolas Gallery, in collaboration with Dwan Gallery, Los Angeles, 1965. Introduction by K. G. Hultèn.

Paris, Musée des Arts Décoratifs (Trois Sculpteurs: César, Roël d'Haese, Tinguely), 1965.

Sao Paolo, Brazil (Machines de Jean Tinguely), Swiss Representation to the VIII Bienal, 1965. Preface by Franz Meyer.

Articles

Apollo, Review of exhibition of recent works at the Galerie Edouard Loeb. v. 65:302. July, 1957.

Apollo, Tinguely at the Galerie Iris Clert. v. 70:30. August, 1959.

Apollo, Tinguely at the Kaplan Gallery. v. 70:132. November, 1959.

Art News, "Theatrical Event at Maidman Theater." v. 61:53. Summer, 1962.

Arts, Review of exhibition at Staempfli Gallery, v. 34:55–6. March, 1960.

Arts, Review of exhibition at Staempfli Gallery, v. 35:89. May, 1961.

Ashbery, John, "Paris Sculptors. New Generations Create Striking New Forms." *Art News Annual,* No. 30:140–159, 175–176, 179–180, 1965.

Ashton, Dore, "Art: Machine-like Work." *New York Times,* January 28, 1960.

Ashton, Dore, "Prologue and Log." *Arts and Architecture,* v. 77: 18–19. May, 1960.

Ashton, Dore, "L'Art Européen à New York." *XXe Siècle,* ns. 22: sup. 22. June, 1960.

Ashton, Dore, "Die selsame maschine des Monsieur Tinguely." *Baukunst und Werkform,* v. 14:90–2. February, 1961.

Ashton, Dore, Review of exhibition at Staempfli Gallery. *Arts and Architecture,* v. 78:5. June, 1961.

Aujourd'hui, Exposition à Genève, v. 8:89. July, 1964.

Berg, Paul, *St. Louis Post Dispatch.* March 6, 1959.

Bordier, Roger, Review of Exhibition at Galerie Arnaud. *Art d'Aujourd'hui,* Ser. 5, No. 4–5:62. May-June, 1954.

Bordier, Roger, Review of exhibition at Galerie Arnaud. *Art d'Aujourd'hui,* Ser. 5, No. 7:30. November, 1954.

Boudaille, George, "Jean Tinguely." *Cimaise,* 9th yr., No. 60:52–59. July-August, 1962.

Brookner, A., Review of exhibition at the Galerie Rive Droite. *Burlington Magazine,* v. 104:45. January, 1962.

Buchwald, Art, *New York Herald Tribune.* June 3, 1959.

Burckhardt, L., "Anti-design, zu einer demonstration von Jean Tinguelys wassersprühern in Baden." *Das Werk,* v. 49: sup. 260. November, 1962.

Burlington Magazine, Sculpture at Staempfli Gallery, v. 102:132. March, 1960.

Butler, Barbara, "Monet and others: a New York Letter." *Art International,* v. IV/4:69. May, 1960.

Byron, William R., "Wacky Artist of Destruction." *Saturday Evening Post,* pp. 76–79. April 21, 1962.

Canaday, John, "Machine Tries to Die for Its Art." *New York Times.* March 18, 1960.

Canaday, John, "Odd Kind of Art, Thoughts on Destruction and Creation After a Suicide in a Garden." *New York Times.* March 27, 1960.

Cianett, Franco, "Tinguely." *Du,* No. 278:27–43. April, 1964.

Coates, Robert M., "Art Galleries." *New Yorker,* v. 35:119–20. February 13, 1960.

Conil-Lacoste, Michel, *Le Monde.* November 21, 1958.

Conil-Lacoste, Michel, "Tinguely is he a Sculptor?" *Studio International,* v. 169:88–91. February, 1965.

Courthion, Pierre, "Tinguely, la sculpture saisie par la machine." *Arts,* Paris, No. 1.001:4–5. June 23-July 6, 1965.

Das Werk, "Kricke, Luginbuhl, Tinguely in der Berner Kunsthalle." v. 47: sup. 220–1. November, 1960.

Descargues, Pierre, "Les Nouvelles Machines de Jean Tinguely." *XXe Siècle.* June, 1965.

Dorfles, G., "L'Oggetto nella Pittura: Mostra alla Galleria Schwarz a Milano." *Domus,* No. 377:40. April, 1961.

Dornand, Guy, *Liberation.* July 30, 1959.

Du, Yr. 19, No. 222:52–53. August, 1959.

Factor, Don, Review of Exhibition at Dwan Gallery. *Artforum,* v. 2, No. 3:14, 17. September, 1963.

Ferebee, A., "On the Move." *Industrial Design,* 11: 63. February, 1964

Gassiot-Talabot, Gerald, "Lettre de Paris," Exhibition at Iolas Gallery, *Art International,* v. IX/2:38. March, 1965.

Genauer, Emily, Arts and Books Review, *New York Herald Tribune.* January, 1961.

Habasque, Guy, Exhibition at the Galerie Edouard Loeb. *Aujourd'hui,* Yr. 3, No. 13:28. June, 1957.

Habasque, Guy, "Art et Technique, La Cinétique." *XXe Siècle,* ns. 23:87. December, 1961.

Habasque, Guy, "XIXe Salon de Mai." *L'Oeil,* No. 102:28. June, 1963.

Hahn, Otto, "Les Méta-mécaniques." *L'Express,* No. 704. December 14–20, 1964.

Henningsen, Paul, "Tinguely." *Mobilia,* Special No., 1962.

Hess, Thomas B., Review of "Homage to New York" at the Museum of Modern Art, New York. *Art News,* 59:16+. April, 1960.

Hultèn, K. G., "Une Sculpture-Machine de Tinguely pour les Lecteurs de Metro." *Metro,* No. 6:60–61. June, 1962.

Industrial Design, "Put Another Nickel In." v. 7:24. March, 1960.

Jouffroy, Alain, "Tinguely," *Combat,* May, 1960.

Kroll, Jack, Review of exhibition at Staempfli Gallery. *Art News,* 60: 14. May, 1961.

Kroll, Jack, Review of exhibition at Iolas Gallery. *Art News,* 61:11. January, 1963.

Lévêque, Jean-Jacques, "Procès de l'Automatisme." *Sens Plastique,* No. VIII. October, 1959.

L'Express, Review of exhibition at Musée des Arts Décoratifs. June 28-July 4, 1965.

Linde, Ulf, "Tinguely Strenghed." *Louisiana Revy,* No. 1. September, 1961.

Lippard, Lucy, R. "New York Letter." *Art International,* V. IX/4:58. May, 1965.

Lundkvist, Artur, "Rörelse i Konsten." *BLM,* No. 7. September, 1961.

Marchand, Sabine, "Cèsar, Tinguely et Röel d'Haese au Musée des Arts Décoratifs." *Le Figaro,* July 1, 1965.

Mathews, Laura, "The Design for Motion of Jean Tinguely: a portfolio and interview." *The Paris Review,* No. 34:83–6, 1965.

Michelson, Annette, Paris Letter, Exhibition at Iolas Gallery, *Art International,* v. IX/2:40. March, 1965.

Morschel, J., "Maschinen, Larm und spiel: Ausstellung im Stedelijkmuseum." Das Kunstwerk, v. 14:80. April, 1961.

Nation, "Tinguely's Contraption." Editorial comment. 190:267. March 26, 1960.

Netter, M., "Ausstellung in Basel." *Das Werk,* v. 49: sup. 68. March, 1962.

Nordland, Gerald, "Neo-Dada Goes West." *Arts,* v. 36:102. May, 1962.

Pease, Jr., Roland F., "New York Notes." *Art International,* v. V/5–6: 96. June-August, 1961.

Peillex, George, "Jean Tinguely et la Méta-mécanique." *Style,* No. 1, 1961.

Peillex, George, Exposition à Genéve. *Das Werk,* v. 51: sup. 158. July, 1964.

Peillex, George, "L'Anti-Machine a l'Exposition nationale à Lausanne." *Das Werk,* v. 51:259–61. July, 1964.

Preston, Stuart, "Machine called Homage to New York at The Museum of Modern Art." *Burlington Magazine,* v 102:229. May, 1960.

Preston, Stuart, "Construction and Sculpture at the Staempfli Gallery." *Burlington Magazine,* v. 103:293. July, 1961.

Raynor, V., Review of exhibition at Iolas Gallery. *Arts,* v. 37:54. January, 1963.

Restany, Pierre, Exposition à la Galerie Denise René, *Cimaise,* 4th ser., No. 2:36. November-December, 1956.

Restany, Pierre, "Die Beseelung des objektes." *Das Kunstwerk,* v. 15:38. July, 1961.

Restany, Pierre, "Tinguely." *XXe Siècle,* ns. 24, No. 19, sup: 20–1. June, 1962.

Restany, Pierre, "Le nouveau réalisme und was darunter zu verstehen ist." *Das Kunstwerk,* vol. 16, No. 7, sup: 1–18. January, 1963.

Restany, Pierre, "La Torre-segnale, alla fiera di Losanna: una grande macchina di Jean Tinguely." *Domus,* No. 415:14–15. June, 1964.

Restany, Pierre, "Un maitre du réalisme fantastique: Jean Tinguely." *Planète,* March-April, 1965.

Reutersvärd, Oscar, and Fahlström, Oyvind, "Jean Tinguely: Luftleken och krosshammaren." *Konstrevy* (Stockholm), No. 5–6: 192–196, 197–201. December, 1960.

Richter, Hans, "Exposition du Mouvement à Amsterdam." *Aujourd'hui,* ser. 5, No. 31:54–5. May, 1961.

Rickey, George, "Kinetic International." *Arts,* v. 35:16–21. September, 1961.

Schubert, H., "Kunstausstellungen im Rheinland." *Das Kunstwerk,* v. 14:74. November, 1960.

Schubert, H., "Die bildende kunst im Gelsenkirchener theater." *Das Kunstwerk,* v. 14:27. January, 1961.

Seckler, Dorothy G., "Audience is his medium." *Art in America,* vol. 51, No. 2:62–67. April, 1963.

Secunda, Arthur, "Two motion sculptors: Tinguely and Rickey." *Artforum,* vol. 1, No. 1:16–18. June, 1962.

Shepherd, Michael, Review of exhibition at Kaplan Gallery. *Art News and Reviews* (London), No. 20:7, 10. October 24, 1959.

Thabit, Walter, *The Village Voice* (New York). March 30, 1960.

Thwaites, John A., "Reaching the Zero Zone." *Arts,* v. 36:16–21. September, 1962.

Time Magazine, "Jangling Man." v. 73:72. March 30, 1959.

Time Magazine, "Homage to New York?" v. 75:86. March 28, 1960.

Tinguely, Jean, "Designs for Motion" (with Laura Mathews). *The Paris Review,* No. 34:83–6. 1965.

Tomkins, Calvin, "A Profile of Jean Tinguely: Beyond the Machine." *New Yorker,* pp. 44–93. February 10, 1962. Later reprinted in a somewhat altered form in *The Bride and the Bachelors,* The Viking Press, New York, 1965.

Tono, Ichiyanagui, "Jean Tinguely." *Mizue,* No. 699:53–59. May 1963.

Tono, Yoshiaki, *Mizue,* 1961.

Tono, Yoshiaki, *The Geijutsu-Shincho,* No. 5, 1963.

Tono, Yoshiaki, *Painting,* No. 4, 1964.

van der Waals, J. C., "Dada Rediviva." *Museum Journal,* ser. 6, No. 9/10, Stedelijk van Abbee Museum, Eindhoven; Rijksmuseum Kroller-Muller, Otterlo; Stedelijkmuseum, Amsterdam. April-May, 1961.

Watts, A., "Paris Commentary." *Studio,* v. 157:26–7. January, 1959.

Watts, A. "Paris Letter. Trends and Coming Events." *Art in America,* v. 47, no. 4:110. (Winter, 1959.)

Watts, A. "Group of neo-realists." *Studio,* v. 161:146. April, 1961.

Watts, A. "Paris Letter: Nouveaux Réalistes." *Art in America,* v. 49, No. 2:112. 1961.

Wescher, Herta, "Die 'neuen realisten' und ihre vorläufer." *Das Werk,* v. 49:293–4. August, 1962.

Films

Brinkley Journal. 1961. National Broadcasting Company, Inc. Television. 28 mins.

La Fin du Monde. 1962. National Broadcasting Company, Inc. Television. Filmed in the Nevada desert in color. 28 mins.

Program on Tinguely's work produced by M. Lachaise. 1963. Télévision Suisse. 40 mins.

Program on Tinguely's work. 1963. Hiroshi Teshigahara, Japan. 15 mins.

Program on Tinguely's work. 1964. British Broadcasting Corporation. Television. 45 mins.